"Corey createc The information and insights in *HIT HAPPENS* are not only valuable, but come from someone who has spent years actually being and doing the things he has written about. And, *HIT HAPPENS* is easy and fun to read! If you are (or think you want to be) a Songwriter, do yourself a favor: read it, mark in it, highlight it, keep it handy, and use it as a reference manual! I highly recommend this book and its Author!" --**Kenny Angel**, Executive Director of Tennessee Songwriter Association International

"This is amazing! I'm so proud of Corey! He has been writing songs since he was a very young lad. His sense of humor is excellent. This is a book that I would recommend to not just new songwriters, but to seasoned professionals as well. I think everyone would get a good laugh at various parts…. I've known Corey for quite a while, and the first two words that come to my mind are 'honesty' and 'integrity.'" – **Linda Lucchesi**, CEO/President, Simply Grand Music, Inc., Sounds of Memphis

"Corey Barker is without question one of the most talented and unique songwriters, period ....Over the years that I have known him, and written with him, he never ceases to amaze me with the way he continually writes 'hit quality' songs from what appears to be a never-ending supply of lyrics and melodies. And now he has written this book filled with vital information from the years of experience and knowledge he has acquired on his music journey. *HIT HAPPENS* will not only guide you step by step on what it takes to be a successful songwriter, it will put a smile on your face while you're learning. Happy reading. Happy learning from someone who is not only talented and honest, but one of my best songwriting friends!" –**Anita Cox**, Singer/Songwriter/Project Concept & Development Specialist, CEO Big South Productions, BobbyCyrusEntertainment.com

"Corey Barker...defines the word 'crazy'... he has one of those comedic brains...which lends itself to the songwriter. In him...that makes for an explosive combination to create one of the best songwriters I've ever been around in my nearly 40 years in the music business....!!!" --**Jim Cartwright**, CEO of Fame and Fortune Entertainment

"Great stuff. Many laugh out loud moments."
--**Kimo Forrest**, CEO of Ohana Music Group

"In many ways Corey reminds me of myself. I swear it's like looking in a mirror sometimes!" --**Corey Lee Barker**, Songwriter and Author

"Corey is a man of integrity. His experience and talent as a songwriter are invaluable. In the process of developing an artist and preparing them for a demo or CD I often reach out to Corey who works tirelessly to write customized songs for each artist and their project. His knowledge of the music industry is vast. With *HIT HAPPENS*, Corey is giving songwriters a pattern and the insight to skills he has gathered throughout his professional career. It's a must read for all songwriters."
--**Regina Boy Carter**, President of Tri-Star Entertainment and Management Group

# HIT
# HAPPENS

Your
Beginner's
Q and A
Guide
to
Nashville
Songwriting

Three Kings Publishing

Hit Happens: Your Beginner's Q and A Guide to Nashville
Songwriting

ISBN  978-0-6924-4805-2

Cover Art by SelfPubBookCovers.com/finecomm

Three Kings Publishing
115 Canterbury Court
Princeton, Kentucky 42445
threekingspublishing@gmail.com

A portion of every Three Kings book sale is given to support
education through the nonprofit Future Hope Africa.

# HIT HAPPENS

Your

Beginner's

Q and A

Guide

to

Nashville

Songwriting

by Corey Lee Barker

# Introduction

In a world where everybody and their grandmother believes they are a professional songwriter and where self-help songwriting books are sprouting up like wild hairs on bigfoot's arm pits, I bet it's nice to finally find a book that is actually helpful and pleasantly informative. After you get done reading that book please read this one too.

With over 400 cuts in various genres such as Country, Christian, Pop/Rock, Reggae, Polka, Comedy, TV and film I feel like I have a few ideas that may help you in your journey to gain recognition and have your songs heard. If all of my ideas suck and my answers are as useful as earphones on a deaf monkey at least the book is short and you didn't waste too much time.

In this book I will attempt to break down some of the questions that beginning songwriters have to help them get to the next step. In a basic question and answer format I've tried to answer the most frequently asked questions that I encounter. Usually those answered start with humor and then transition into a serious answer.

I've done my best to keep the content on a level where a 4th grader could understand it. Not that I feel you need that much help but rather because my intellect can be rivaled by the average nine year old and I don't want to confuse myself or others who may be counting on me.

I've had the pleasure of helping several hundred up and coming writers over the years and most have similar questions that I felt like addressing in a book before I'm too old to remember the answers.

I absolutely do not have ALL the answers or I would be filthy rich. I have, however, been blessed with multiple cuts on recording artist albums, television, movies, etc. I'd love to share some of my methods, knowledge, and good luck stories with you. It would do my heart good if anything I have learned can help you get closer to your dream.

Here are some of the questions I've been asked along with some sarcastic answers for your entertainment. Make sure you read the real answer after that or you may think I'm a heartless son of a biscuit.

# Author's Suggestions

*You should only read this book if you are tired, wide awake, married, single, or pooping.*

*Don't skip to page 78 because you might miss the first 77 pages.*

*Read it twice in case the lights were off the first time.*

*Share this information with people you know, people you don't know, and irritating people you wish you didn't know.*

*Buy four copies in case you lose one, one gets stolen, and you spill buttermilk on the 3rd while skating through the house blind folded before losing control after tripping on a log. Believe me I've seen this a hundred times!*

# Disclaimer:

*Since the music business changes every five minutes the information in this book will probably be incorrect by the time you get a copy so why are you still reading?*

*Seriously stop reading!*

*Do you not understand the words coming out of my mouth?*

*You are so stubborn!*

*Fine. But don't say I didn't warn you.*

# CONTENTS

How do you handle criticism?

How do I know which critics I should trust and which ones I should disregard?

Does it matter how long the intro to my song is?

What if my computer crashes and I lose all my songs?

Should I avoid listening to the radio so I'll always be original?

Should I save my songs for only the high profile artists?

Is there such a thing as morality when it comes to songwriting?

When I do a demo...why do I need to ask for a copy of the tracks without vocals as well?

## PART THREE
### How Can I Break Into the Scene?

Why should I bother networking?

What are cuts and how do I get some?

Is co-writing really that helpful?

How do I know my demo is good enough?

What is a ghost writer?

What is a pitch and when is it appropriate?

What are some tips to make my pitch go as smoothly as possible?

What is a plugger?

What is publishing in the songwriting business?

Should I enter every songwriting contest I can find to help further my career?

I'm familiar with the CMA and ACM award shows but recently I've heard of ICM as well. Can you tell me anything about that?

## PART FOUR
### How Will I Get Paid?

Do I really need to sign up at BMI, ASCAP, or SESAC? And if I do…which is better?

What is a staff deal?

I am now signed up with a PRO. When and how do I get royalty checks?

When do I need to copyright my songs?

Do I need to register my work before or after it's a hit?

When do I stop getting paid on my hit song?

How much can I make by writing a parody of a famous song?

How do I figure out what percentage of the song is mine if I wrote most of it and someone else helped out slightly?

Does it make sense to search for an investor?

## PART FIVE

## Do I Have What It Takes?

What if I want to be a writer but I don't play an instrument or I'm great at music but I'm not naturally a lyricist?

What are the odds that I can make a living writing songs?

I haven't had any success and I've been at it for a while. When should I give up?

## PART SIX
## What Technical Terms Do I Need to Know?

What does it mean if I get a song "on hold"?

What is a single song contract?

What are sharks?

What is a work tape and how is it different form a demo?

I heard a writer talking about writing up. What does that mean?

## PART SEVEN
## How Can I Hold On To My Dream?

Should I set goals or just write and see what happens?

What is a retreat?

I spend all my free time trying to make it happen and often get frustrated as success seems so improbable. What do I do?

I have writer's block. Any suggestions?

When can I tell everyone about my cut?

My song is ready to come to life. Who should I choose to demo it?

Should I play my songs at writer's nights?

Would it be helpful for me to join a writer's organization?

I need to concentrate on my music. It's not possible to work a real job and still write songs is it?

## PART EIGHT

### What About TV Shows, Movies and Youtube?

What is a TV track?

How do I get my song in a TV show or movie?

Can I make money off of my Youtube videos? How?

# PART ONE

What Are the Essentials of
Writing a Hit Song?

# Do I need a certain attitude to be successful in my songwriting career?

*It's important to believe that you are the best ever and your poo poo doesn't stink. No one can hold a candle next to your extreme abilities. Jeffrey Steele, Craig Wiseman, Dianne Warren, and Skip Ewing should be lucky to call themselves songwriters when standing in the shadows of your greatness. You are the Shiznit and should be worshipped as such.*

*If you believe this then you should also believe I was a unicorn in a past life who married an alien named Bob who suffered from anorexia three years prior to his Super bowl MVP performance at age four.*

You might ask what in the Sam Elliot does attitude have to do with songwriting? Well, just about everything. First of all you are already fighting an uphill battle against a few hundred thousand other people who have the same goal in mind.

If your attitude is anything other than, "I am going to be successful no matter how long it takes," then you will be miserable for...well...ever.

Next you have to remember that attitude towards yourself and your talents are only part of it. The attitude you have towards others is vital as well. If you treat others in the industry with professionalism and courtesy then you will develop a sense of comradery and trust that can come in handy in many situations. When you need a door opened those same individuals may very well hold the key.

The biblical golden rule - do unto others as you'd have them to unto you - regardless of your personal beliefs, can come in very handy in the music business as well. Treat others as you would like to be treated. Publishers, other writers, labels, etc. enjoy dealing with people who are easy to work with.

Of course continually delivering quality work doesn't hurt either.

# What is the best way to begin a song?

*The best way to begin a song is to write something at the top of the page. Keep writing until you run out of room at the bottom and then you are finished.*

The answer to this is that there's no set answer. The most popular way is to start with the hook. Every line in the song is supposed to support the hook so it only stands to reason that it's a great place to start. There are other writers who like to play around on the guitar or piano until a melody comes to mind and then let the lyric build itself around the mood.

Typically when I co-write we all come to the session with certain song ideas. After throwing them all out on the table we go with the one that collectively hits us the hardest, and then we let the magic begin. I have other co-writing friends that only write music, and in those cases I like to put a disc of their music in my jeep and drive around until the vibe spits out a title I'm compelled to jump on.

Very seldom do I start writing a lyric around a story without yet knowing what the hook or title will be, but it has happened before.

I read somewhere that Bobby Pinson doesn't start writing the first lyric until he has finished creating a commercial melody. If you've listened to Sugarland or Toby Keith for the last few years you've heard his writing.

# Is the range of my melody of any importance?

*No. Everyone can sing five octaves so be creative!*

This is something not talked about much but definitely worth thinking about. If you are writing for Carrie Underwood or Martina McBride a song without much of a range may not be very appealing to them. There are some artists, such as these, who like to showcase their ability to vocally explode and a song with a low range such as *Margaritaville* may not be of much use to them.

On the flipside if you write a song with too much of a range you may rule out 90% of vocalists in the business. My advice is, unless you are writing for a specific person, let the song go where it wants to and figure out who can cut it later.

# What is modulation and is it really important?

*Modulation is when you have a snot wad stuck in your throat and it keeps coming up and going back down creating a flimsy gargling sound and a need for you to cough.*

A modulation is when the key of a song changes up a half step or more. You see this most often in power ballads right after the bridge coming into the 3rd chorus. Although it helps lift the emotional level in some songs, it's not always necessary and in certain songs it can be overkill. I tend to lean toward the overkill, so I rely on my co-writers to say "not this time modulation king."

# How important is the song's title?

*Not important at all. Please write another "I love you" or "without you" song so my life will be complete. Don't be offended if you already have because I'm guilty as well.*

About a year after I moved to town I was having a conversation with a writer who had multiple number ones in the 60's and 70's. As a matter of fact he's had over 200 major cuts. He told me if he's ever heard the title before he won't even pick up his pencil and start on the song.

I don't take it to that extreme but I do take that concept to heart. I always check BMI.com and do a title search before I begin a song. If there are very few or none by that title I get much more motivated. As the years go by it is more and more difficult to come up with original titles, but I believe it's our creative duty to try whenever we can.

Here's a personal heart break example: In 2003 I was in the office of a record label exec playing a song I wrote a few years prior called *You Are*. Halfway through the chorus another A&R rep came barging in and asked, "Where did you get that song?"

As it turns out he had gotten a hold of my song months before and wanted to cut it as a duet on a famous act and a newcomer. He searched BMI to find out who wrote it and there were over 700 songs by that title so he could not find the answer to get clearance. They ultimately ended up doing another song. I was devastated but learned a very valuable lesson about original titles.

Also keep in mind that on any given day a label's exec may have 100 CD's on their desk or more. If you were sitting at a desk and saw three CD's that were titled, *You Are Great, She's Gone*, and *My Give a Damn's Busted*...which one would you listen to? Me too, and that's one of the reasons it became a huge hit for Jodee Messina. Interesting titles almost demand that the song be listened to. By the way Joe Diffie recorded that song a few years before Jodee Messina did and was a co-writer. I'm not sure what that has to do with anything but I love Joe Diffie.

# Is it better to use hard or soft rhymes?

*Soft rhymes are better since the paper you write the lyrics on won't weigh as much.*

Many writers have different opinions on this. I have written with writers that refuse to do a soft rhyme as if it's a cop out. I have written with others who refuse to use a hard rhyme because they think it's too predictable. I tend to be somewhere in the middle, although I lean more towards the soft rhymes because I like the option of being more creative. Sometimes it's ok to make up a word as long as it makes sense to everyone without having to explain it (i.e. - chillaxin, fangasmic, mamaliscious). Roger Miller may have my favorite when he rhymed purple with maple syruple. I don't recommend going that far outside of the box but he had that humorous personality where he could get away with it.

# Is there any harm in using a rhyming dictionary?

*Of course not. Who wants to use their brain?*

The answer is, unfortunately, no. I personally try to stay away from them if at all possible as I feel like I'm cheating myself. However I admit it is better than forcing a trite rhyme, and for that reason I don't rule out the possibility. There are moments when we have to sacrifice our pride for the betterment of the creation.

# How do I know when my song is too long?

*The moment when the last person in the audience passes out or commits suicide because they can't take it anymore.*

Although there are exceptions, for example *Almost Home* by Craig Morgan, the typical kiss of death for radio play is the four minute mark. Do your best to keep your song under that mark if possible. However if you are absolutely convinced you are sacrificing a piece of the story to fit a standard you don't believe in, then go with what your gut says.

# Do the same rules apply for writing pop hits as for country?

*Yes, because Michael Jackson and Willie Nelson often enjoyed trading songs and outfits before moonwalking at their concerts.*

This info is from the number one songs of 2012 (the year I started writing this book) and was a result of former NSAI president Ralph Murphy's research.

Let's start with POP.

1) 80% of all pop hits are written using the same structure:

> VERSE
> CHORUS
> PRE-CHORUS
> VERSE 2
> PRECHROUS
> CHORUS
> BRIDGE
> FINAL CHRORUS
> TAG OR ALTRO.

2) At least 2/3 of all pop hits last year were at 100 beats per minute or more (so think mid to up-tempo)

3) 20 percent of number one writers are women.

4) Almost all the pop hits used the pronoun you within 20 seconds as it invites the listener in.

5) The bridge happens somewhere between the 2 minute and 2 and a half minute mark.

6) The Title is repeated 7 times on average.

7) Intro is 8 seconds long on average.

## COUNTRY

1) Almost 3 times the number ones that were on the pop charts. This is a result of pop songs taking longer to fall off the charts. This is good news for the pop writers' paychecks. On the flip side it means there are more opportunities to have a number one country hit.

Note: in the ICM market the charts only come out once a month so you have 12 chances at a number one hit as opposed to 52.

2) Around 2/3 of the artists were co-writers on their songs.

3) 2/3 of the hits were under 100 beats per minute.

4) 75% of the number one songs were performed by male artists.

5) Of the 80 writers on number one songs only 7 were women.

6) Average intro length was 14 seconds

7) Again almost all used the pronoun you within 20 seconds

8) Almost all number ones got to the title in 60 seconds or less

**Note**: Both genres use the word "you" in place of her or him. A few years after I moved to town I had a conversation with Award winning producer Scotty Turner who told me he strongly believed this very same thing. He said no lady wants to hear you sing about someone else.

By singing to her and using the word "you" she can put herself in that place and fantasize that the song was written specifically for her and not for your past or present love interest. Made sense to me and still does.

# PART TWO

## What Are the Biggest Do's and Don'ts For Songwriters?

# How can I sell my song and how much should I ask for it?

*Go to Craigslist and search for the heading, "Would love to buy your song for $100 and cheat you out of all future royalties for the rest of your life and beyond." Contact that person immediately and then retire.*

One of the funniest questions I get on a regular basis is, "How many songs have you sold lately?"

There is rarely ever a time when someone "sells" a song outright. I have sold my publishing portion to a particular song or two before but never all of my writer's portion as well. Think about that for a minute.

Let's say you sold all the rights to your song for $500 because you needed to pay rent. Then it becomes a number one country song, a pop cross over, and gets placed on the movie sound track of *Die Hard 85* and brings in $4 million. The residuals you would get for that future income would be a whopping zero dollars and zero cents. If you had sold only the publishing rights for $250 and kept your writer's portion you would have brought home $2 million that year. Which do you think would have been the smarter choice? Please don't sell your song.

# Is it really so wrong to bootleg?

*Is it really so wrong to put razor blades in kids' candy at Halloween?*

"Bootlegging" is the unauthorized recording and selling of a song. It's been happening for many decades and it does not make the publishers and songwriters giggle with glee. Many writers and artists save for months or even years to be able to put their music to CD, and they do not deserve this kind of blatant disrespect. Anyone caught bootlegging should immediately have their car seats replaced with deer antlers.

# How do you handle criticism?

*If anyone finds something wrong with your song they are stupid and need to be hit in the left knee cap 700 times and then have their ear stapled to the bumper of a four wheeler as it blasts its way through poison ivy infested woods.*

Never get angry when someone offers criticism of your music because there are two possibilities:

Either, they are wrong/jealous and you will be able to use their quotes as motivation to prove your worthiness...or...

They are correct and you now have the opportunity to pin point the weakness and make the song stronger with a re-write.

Either way you have to remember it is impossible to please everybody. There are simply too many styles and preferences for everyone to want to buy your tune no matter how wonderful it is.

I was working on a parody album several years back, and I mentioned it to a friend of mine that had a few number one hits recently. He said, "That makes sense. If you can't write hit songs just make fun of everybody else's." I should have been very upset but it actually made me smile inside knowing I can remind him of that one day after my number one party.

# How do I know which critics I can trust and which ones I should disregard?

*Only trust your family and close friends because they are not biased at all and they know everything about the music business. You can also trust the drunk people in karaoke bars because they are great listeners and have sound advice...especially on Thursdays.*

Publishers, producers, and fellow songwriters with years of experience are good people to turn to for evaluations. If several people point out the same flaw then you should probably revisit your song and try to make necessary improvements. In some cases you are right and everyone else is wrong, but those cases are not as common as you would like them to be.

I remember my first critique at a Nashville Songwriters Association International (NSAI) meeting. I was so excited for them to hear my song because there was no way they would find ANTYHING wrong with it. They ripped it to shreds. I was angry and tried to defend it. It didn't take me 30 minutes to realize they were right about every suggestion and I was an idiot.

# Does it matter how long the intro to my song is?

*Not at all.  All producers love hearing a two hour intro. Most Artist and Repertoire (A&R) reps are thrilled to give up a huge chunk of their day for the privilege of basking in anticipation as to what the heck your song is going to be about?*

Keep in mind the first 30 seconds are usually enough to hook the listener or drive them to push eject or change the station. That being said it's a good idea to make sure your demo doesn't have more than a 15 second intro if possible.

# What if my computer crashes and I lose all my songs?

*In that case you are hosed and your dream is dead. Thank you for playing.*

Always keep back-ups. There are two ways I protect my music.

First, always keep hard copies of your material and background tracks. You can usually fit about 20 songs on a disc and that makes it easier to re-download if your computer crashes.

Second, I have a particular email account where I keep all my songs with attached lyric sheets. Always put the name of your song in the subject matter. This way you can search by title and pull it up instantly. This system also makes pitching very simple because the email already has the song, lyric, and contact info attached so you simply have to forward the email.

Some people even go as far as to make additional hardcopies/lyric sheets and leaving them with a friend or family member in case of a fire. This does not sound so odd if you've ever had to recollect your catalog after a computer crash or moving to another home/office.

# Should I avoid listening to the radio so I'll always be original?

*Yes. Also avoid ever speaking because you may say something that has already been said.*

I've heard writers say they never listen to the radio because they don't want to accidentally copy anyone.

I tend to believe that I am MORE likely to copy someone if I don't know what's out there. I also like to be on top of what's being overused so I don't become too trite with my lyrics. I want to know who sings what style and what titles/subject matter they have already covered. It would make no sense to send Luke Bryan a song called *Shake It City Girl* if he already has one called *Country Girl Shake It For Me*.

I don't recommend sleeping with the radio on however. You may subconsciously pick up a melody and use it down the line not knowing that it wasn't yours. Just because it's a forgivable honest mistake doesn't mean it won't cost you half your royalties if the song becomes a hit.

# Should I save my songs for only the high profile artists?

*What if you saved your kisses for only supermodels and you were not super attractive yourself? You may go through life with some very chapped lips and an extremely deflated ego.*

I understand why most major songwriters want to hold out for the Blake Shelton's or Taylor Swift's but in most cases I simply don't agree. Many of those major artists would not be able to stay on top if we only pitched them our mediocre material from now on. In a similar fashion the lesser known artists wouldn't have a chance to become major artists if no one pitched them top drawer songs to compete with. You never know when an indie artist may break though and become a house hold name. It could even be his producer that makes it big and remembers how you pitched him songs when he was an unknown.

I'll tell you the saddest example I know of. A friend of mine had an artist come up to him in the late 80's saying he had just signed a record deal and would love to record some of his material on his debut album. My friend told him that he didn't mean to offend him but he'd have to wait until the artist established himself first and then he would think about it. Well, that artist is a fellow you may have heard of named Garth Brooks who went on to sell over 100 million albums. My friend never got that opportunity again. I refuse to ever be that guy.

# Is there such a thing as morality when it comes to songwriting?

*Morality does not apply to songwriting so please feel free to step on whomever you need to in order to get to the top. If you think I'm serious then I also want to let you know that I am a one armed zombie from the planet Cromagnitanium who was sent here to be the next co-star on Walking Dead.*

If you read nothing else in this book but this tiny section then it was still worth my time to write the whole thing. It's usually easy to know when you are doing the "right thing" in most situations, but just for argument sake let me list a few ways to know you are morally doing the "wrong thing."

The following thoughts are simply my opinions and the punishment suggestions for committing any of these wrong doings could possibly be considered odd in some areas of Alaska and the upper West side of 2nd street in a small town in Canada.

1. *If you steal a friend's song idea, melody or title (on purpose), you should* - have to wrestle an alligator while wearing a T-bone steak strapped to your back. It's important to note that you might steal an idea accidently, so if you realize you've done this contact the writer and ask them if they'd

rather you write a new song or be included as co-writer on yours.

2. *If you don't give credit to your co-writer during writers' nights, TV appearances, or Youtube videos you post, you should -* be forced to breakdance on national TV wearing your grandmother's underwear, roller blades, and a football helmet.

3. *If you get a major staff deal and then ignore the phone calls of everyone you knew before, you should -* have your butt cheeks duck taped together following a visit to an all you can eat Chinese buffet.

4. *If you have a staff deal and you hide some songs from your publisher, you should -* be required to get a tattoo above your left nipple that says, "Hang Christmas ornaments here."

5. *If your co-writer gives you a contact and asks you to pitch some songs you wrote together but you only pitch your own, you should -* spend one night in jail with a guy named Bubba while wearing a pink dress and a shirt that says, "Wham was the best band ever."

6. *If you promised to write a certain song with one writer and don't clear it with them before writing it with a different writer -* it is ok for someone else to clean their toilet with your toothbrush and not tell you about it until two weeks later.

7. *If you talk smack about another writer to a recording artist so you stand a chance of replacing their cut with one of your own, you*

*should* - have a target painted on your forehead while the 5th graders at the nearest elementary school use you as a target for their booger flicking contest.

8. *If you register a song with different percentages than previously agreed upon, you should* - play a game of twister, by yourself, covered in peanut butter, on a hill occupied by fire ants, on a Tuesday.

9. *If you lie about credits (i.e. — Mark Chestnut sang a DEMO for you in 1986 and you post that you have a CUT by Mark Chestnut), you should* - have to sing a solo at church on Easter wearing a diaper with chocolate pudding gushing out the sides.

10. *If you collect the mechanical Royalties for another writer and purposely withhold some money or lie about amount that was paid, you should* - be required to walk up to Trace Adkins, slap him in the face, and call him a sissy.

There are many more examples but I think you get the picture.

# When I do a demo...why do I need to ask for a copy of the tracks without vocals as well?

*Because if you have two CD's instead of one you won't have to buy a coaster for your coffee cup.*

Always specify that you need tracks without vocals for your songs to whoever is producing your demo for many reasons:

1. You may realize the singer sang one of the words wrong or left out an important conjunction that alters the meaning of the song.

2. You may think of phrasing down the line that is stronger than what you had.

3. Let's say you are pitching to Rascal Flats or Keith Urban but your demo singer has a traditional George Strait sound. You may want to put another singer on the song for crossover pitches.

4. You may want to sing the song live at a venue that doesn't have a band.

5. You may want to lease your track to another singer for their album.

In any of those cases you would be out of luck or have to hire the band and studio to make a new track if you forgot to save the music by itself. That's an expensive lesson I learned the hard way in the early 90's.

# PART THREE

## How Can I Break Into the Scene?

# Why should I bother networking?

*Why should I bother wiping my butt if I'm going to poop again later on today?*

Networking is one thing you can't afford to take for granted. "I know too many people in the music business," said no one ever. The more you are out there reminding people you exist the more likely it is that they will remember you when opportunities arise. I try to never let more than two weeks go by with any of my contacts without dropping them an email, phone call, or Facebook message to keep me fresh in their minds.

Showcases and talent contests are a great place to network as there are many producers, managers, and label heads frequenting these events. It never hurts to have a CD of some of your best work always handy just in case.

Let's not forget Cyber Networking as well. Youtube is one of the best things to ever happen to artists with little money for marketing. Just ask Justin Beiber. Sometimes a slide show video to your original song provides another dimension to your pitch. I have used this particular method many times when pitching a song, and it has paid off in certain circumstances. The bigger your Network on Facebook, Myspace, Reverbnation, etc., the more people can hear your songs, the more chances you have at success. For instance, you can find my work at:

Facebook.com/coreyleebarker
Reverbnation.com/coreyleebarker4/songs  (for country)
Reverbnation.com/coreyleebarker  (for Christian)
Reverbnation.com/coreylebarkerchristmas/songs  (for Christmas)
Soundcloud.com/coreyleebarker

# What are "cuts" and how do I get some?

*Cuts are abrasions of the skin. You can get some by running naked through a thorn bush.*

When a recording artist records one of your songs and places it on their album or any internet site for sale, that is known as a "cut." They are what build our resumes, pad our wallets, soothe our egos, and ultimately offer us a chance at tooting our horns at music functions.

I remember the first five years I was in town very well for one simple reason. Every time the topic of what I did came up folks would ask me if I've had any songs cut and I'd have to say "not yet". The amount of shame I felt on the inside would be comparable to losing a fist fight on ESPN to a 90 year old blind lady.

So what can you do to increase your chances of getting cuts?

1. Write great songs.

2. Make your demo sound like a record (read section on DEMO).

3. Subscribe to rowfax.com so you will know when acts are looking for songs and who is producing them. Many of the independent acts will list email addresses so

you can mp3 them your material. Remember the old days when you actually had to mail a CD?

4. Write with recording artists. This is the absolute BEST way to increase your chances. Most artists want to record songs they are a part of creating.

5. Befriend as many producers as you can so they will keep you in the loop when they have a project in the works.

6. Write with writers who have staff deals. That way you know your songs are being professionally pitched.

7. Research artists on the internet and let them know you would love to pitch material for their next project. You would be surprised how many recognizable artists control their Facebook and respond when possible.

8. Land a publishing deal. It never hurts to have someone with connections representing your material. If you're lucky enough the draw may be enough for you to work less and write more. Obviously, that leads to more songs and more chances for success.

# Is co-writing really that helpful?

*You don't need anyone else's help to be original. What could someone else possibly have to say that could trump your intellectual greatness? How could they possibly have a melody that could make the world want to sing along louder than the one you have in your head at the current moment? You are the next Richard Marx meets Billy Joel so act like it and write everything by yourself.*

I heard a story about a gentleman that kept bugging Roger Miller to co-write with him day after day until Roger got fed up with the nagging. Roger finally turned around and said, "Why? Picasso didn't co-paint."

As funny as this alleged statement was I do not agree with that mentality for many reasons.

1. If I co-write with someone it doubles my chances of getting it cut because now his or her connections are working the song as well as mine. If I co-write with two people it triples and so on. Sure the piece of the pie gets smaller but the odds of success go up.

2. If you write all your songs by yourself, inevitably they will start to sound alike. Co-writing gives you opportunities to say things a different way and incorporate the different styles and talents that each musician brings to the table (or couch if you don't have a table).

3. You can work with people who excel in the areas where you are weakest and perhaps use your strengths to build up other writers in the areas in which they are lacking. If your solo song is good, but you know it can be better if you call in "randy rocker" to give it that extra something then please, please, please don't decide not to do it out of pride.

There have been many times when I struggled with "liking" a song a lot but knowing I would "love" it if I called Alfons Kettner, Anita Cox, or Jody Harris in to give it some ear candy chords that were out of my guitar playing abilities. Ultimately you have to ask yourself "would I rather be 100% writer on a very good song or 50%, (even 10%) writer on a masterpiece?" I'll take the masterpiece any day.

4. When success does come you have someone to celebrate with. How cool is it to know that your number one song just changed the lives of multiple families as opposed to just yours.

Keep in mind co-writing is a bit like dating although it's not customary to stick your tongue down their throat. There has to be chemistry between the writers for the magic to work. You can put two of the best writers in the world together, but if they can't relate to each other's styles or agree on lyrics there is no guarantee their song will be any good at all. Conversely you could put two "pretty good" writers who click in a room and all of a sudden you have a wonderful song because they lifted each other up and found a way to capitalize off each other's strengths.

# How do I know my demo is good enough?

*As long as we can almost understand the words and most of the musicians are in key you can consider it radio ready.*

I could spend an hour on this question but I'll try not to. You've often heard the phrase, "you get what you pay for." Very, very true in the music business as in most other cases as well. A cheap mediocre demo does you absolutely no good when you are competing with major publishing companies who are cranking out thousand dollar demos on a daily basis. It would serve you better to have an excellent acoustic vocal versus a six piece band of semi talented musicians with a local karaoke singer on lead vocals. Can you think of a business where presentation is NOT important?

So what makes a solid presentation of a song to a label exec?

1. "A" team musicians (with years of studio experience).

2. Great engineer (with years of studio experience).

3. Top notch vocalist (with years of studio experience).

4. Solid lyric with a catchy melody.

Many people try to skip number 3 and sing the demo themselves to save money. There are very few cases where that's a good idea. The vocal is your icing on the cake and can often times be the ear candy that lures the listener in and excites them. If you can't sing as good as the stars on the radio, please take the time to find someone who can. It is more than worth it to swallow your pride and give your demo the knockout punch it deserves. Think of who you are competing against and do everything you can not to give someone a reason to say 'no'.

When it comes to a ballad it is often okay to do a great piano vocal or guitar vocal which will save you some green in your wallet. Up-tempos, however, are very hard to simulate with just one instrument.

General rule is don't cut corners. Wait until you have the money to do it right rather than marvel in mediocrity.

# What is a ghost writer?

*Sometimes you will be stuck on that one line that will finish the song for hours or even days and it's driving you crazy. Then the ghost of a dead songwriter mysteriously comes out from behind the curtain and whispers that illusive rhyme or idea in your ear and all is well in the universe.*

A "ghost writer" in most cases is a writer who contributed to a song but didn't get credit. Most often they were someone who got paid behind the scenes to make the other writer look good. It could also be the case where a professional writer helped out a novice but did not want his or her name associated with the song, because he believed it was a tad less quality than what is normally expected from him or her.

# What is a pitch and when is it appropriate?

*A Pitch is when the songwriter stands 90 feet away from the intended listener (e.g. recording artist, label head) while wearing cleats and throws their CD at them at a speed of 100 miles per hour.*

A pitch is simply an attempt to sell someone on the idea of recording your song. This normally happens through mp3ing to an email or mailing a CD to the office of the record label, artist, manager, etc.

My favorite, and often the most difficult, way to pitch is an actual sit down meeting where you personally play the song for the artist and see their reaction in person. It's much easier to get a feel of how serious they are about recording your song in an environment like that. In any case it is always professional to get permission before submitting material. Some companies are not allowed to accept unsolicited material so you must respect their policies.

Just as important as knowing when to pitch a song would be the art of knowing when not to pitch a song. Here are some scenarios in which it is not okay to pitch material to the artist:

1. When they are at the urinal at Waffle House.

2. When they are silently praying at the altar during church.

3. When the doctor is delivering their baby.

4. When they are on their honeymoon.

5. At the movie theater during the climax of the film.

6. When you are in your underwear.

7. When they are asleep.

8. At their grandma's funeral.

9. When you forgot to bring the song.

10. After they have said repeatedly, "I never want to hear any of your songs again."

# What are some tips to make my pitch go as smoothly as possible?

*Place a thousand dollar bill in the CD packet along with Dolly Parton's phone number and the address of the nearest Cheesecake Factory.*

1. Ask for permission before sending a CD.

2. Have a label printed on your CD.

3. Include a copy of the lyric sheet.

4. Attach an introductory, "Thank you for your time," cover letter.

5. Make sure your contact info is on both the lyric sheet and the CD (in case they get separated).

# What is a plugger?

*A plugger is someone with a cork in his hand who stands behind people at Mexican restaurants who have had a second helping of beans. This is in the best interest of everyone breathing.*

A plugger is actually someone who holds the distinguished and ever challenging job of aggressively finding a home for your song. They scout which artists are looking for which types of songs at the moment and they do their best to get the song that fits that criteria into the hands of someone who can make it happen. These are people you want to have as your best friends. Give them gifts, stroke their ego, and tell them their mother is beautiful whenever you can.

Many pluggers work for set monthly rates while others work off a percentage of the publishing if they get something cut. It's up to you or your publisher to find the scenario that best suits you.

# What is publishing in the song writing business?

*Publishing was derived from the word "pubfishing" in the late 1900's. It used to be common among fraternities to go searching (fishing) for a list of beers from pub to pub until you drank each one on your scavenger list. Hence the term "pubfishing." One day a reporter asked one of these intoxicated gentleman what they were doing and he couldn't enunciate properly so she thought he said, "publishing." That reporter was writing a song at the moment and the idea for publishing was born. This could be why there are so many drinking songs.*

I used to believe the word "publishing" was created by someone in history, possibly named Alfred H. Publishing, who did not know how to write songs but wanted to make as much money as the songwriter. He got together with a council consisting of himself and decided that when a song is created it is immediately divided into two halves:

The writers portion (50%).

And the publishing portion (50%).

I always found this to be rather odd because in any other business if someone makes a sale for you they get a 3% or maybe even a 10% commission. In music it's 50%.

Furthermore, let's say you wrote a song with two other guys signed to the same publisher and it brought in a million dollars. The writers who created the masterpiece would get $167,000 each (roughly) and their publisher, who took 14 seconds out of their day to mp3 the song on their computer, would get half a million!

So what's the advantage of having a publisher you might ask?

There are many:

1. For one thing if you didn't have the contacts to get that song cut then that $167,000 is looking smoking hot and you should be kissing that publisher's feet right now.

2. Many publishers can set you up with other hit writers you didn't have access to.

3. If you're lucky you may get a draw/salary paid to you by a publisher so you can focus on your craft and "live the dream."

4. In many cases the publisher will pay for the demo if they believe in the song enough. If you can't afford to demo then you can write a thousand great songs and they'd be useless.

5. You can't be two places at once. If you are writing eight hours a day, you can't be pitching your music eight hours a day. You need someone working just as hard on the business end of things as you are on the creative end.

6. When it comes down to contract or licensing time and you are not familiar with the terms you may severely short change yourself or ask for way too much and lose the contract.

# Should I enter every songwriting contest I can find to help further my career?

*Should you enter every lottery you can to help further your bank account? The odds aren't much different and the rewards are astronomically less.*

Unfortunately, there are many songwriting contests out there whose sole purpose is to collect your money. Many of these companies feed off ambitious young writers who can't wait to tell their family and friends they won a songwriting contest even though their song may never even get listened to. Some of these contests are even set up by publishing companies or writers who are looking to steal your ideas and rewrite them.

There are many exceptions to these scenarios and it's unfortunate that some of these organizations ruin it for the honest ones. The best thing to do is research the contest and perhaps contact some of the previous winners. If no previous winners can be found I would run in the opposite direction as fast as you can and save your money for demos.

I'm familiar with the CMA and ACM award shows but recently I've heard of ICM as well. Can you tell me anything about that?

*ICM stands for Irritated Cookie Monster. On one of the episodes of Sesame Street the producer stole a cookie off Cookie Monsters plate and he became outraged. He assumed it was Big Bird and punched him in the ear. He made it all better with a nice big hug after finding out he was incorrect and all was good in the Sesame Hood once again.*

ICM is actually one of my favorite organizations. It stands for Inspirational Country Music. Any song with a positive message has a shot. Most of the artists are very approachable and willing to listen to music you may have for them so don't be afraid to email. They have their own charts in Power Source Magazine that come out monthly and their own annual televised awards show as well. Many artists in this genre have been kind enough to record music of mine such as Tommy Brandt, Hunter Cook, Mary James, Charee White, DC Riggs, Aubree Bullock, Adrienne Haupt, Emily Faith, and Mikayla Lynn.

They don't discriminate when it comes to age, gender, race, or beauty. They simply exist to provide the world good music with messages any parent would feel comfortable having their children listen to. It's an honor to be part of the team.

Please check them out at Familyfaithcountry.com

# PART FOUR

## How Will I Get Paid?

# Do I really need to sign up at BMI, ASCAP, or SESAC? And if I do...which is better?

*No need to sign up with either. It's much more fun to cash imaginary checks for your songs being played on radio or any live performance venue.*

Yes you need to pick one. Broadcast Music Incorporated (BMI), American Society of Composers, Authors and Publishers (ASCAP), and Society of European Stage Authors and Composers (SESAC) are your three choices if you want to get paid for performance royalties.

I know many writers who swear by each of them so it's up to you to visit and see which one you feel the most comfortable using. I've been with BMI for 15 years, and it's always a wonderful feeling to open the mailbox each quarter and see a check from them with my name on it. I have no doubt that I would have the same feeling with the other two organizations as well.

As a side note, it is mandatory that you and your publisher both belong to the same PRO in order to get paid. If your publisher is ASCAP but you are a BMI writer you will not be able to register the song. This is why many publishers have more than one company so that they can represent writers of all affiliations. I experienced this when I wrote for Stockbridge Records. Their publishing company was ASCAP. They had to open a BMI company called Stockbridge Publishing so we could register all the songs I wrote when I was with them. If you're not familiar with their breakout artist Barry Michael give him a google. Our military song changed both our lives for the better.

# What is a staff deal?

*A Staff Deal is when everyone you work with (the entire staff) throws a deck of 52 cards on the table at the same time. The last person to find an ace gets slapped in the face with a 12 pound raw fish, receives a wedgie, recites the National Anthem in Spanish, and then has their head shaved. The video gets put on Youtube immediately for all to enjoy.*

To say you have a staff deal means you are lucky enough to have a publishing company that believes in you so much they claim you as one of their writers. The number of these opportunities has drastically dwindled in the last decade due to declining sales of records and increasing internet piracy of our music.

If a publishing company signs you to a staff deal hopefully they are paying you a draw. A draw is a monthly income you are paid in exchange for the publishing portion of your songs. If you end up having a hit or getting a cut, the draw money will be reimbursed to the publisher before you get your royalty check.

A typical draw seems to currently be in the ballpark of $500 a week. There have been times I've made double that and there have been times I've made a fraction of that. In any case it's good to keep a grateful attitude. Most people never make any money doing what they love so consider yourself one of the lucky ones if and when that happens.

There are many different ways staff deals can be structured as well. Most staff deals require the publishing of your best 12 songs (their choice) over the course of the year. If you have a co-writer this could be considered half a song. That would mean you need to turn in 24 songs. Other staff deals may require a different number or even ALL of your songs. It just depends on what you and the PRO are comfortable with in any case.

On a side note it's good to have somewhere in the contract how many songs they will be demoing. If you have nothing to pitch and not much of a draw it may not be worth your time. Remember to have a lawyer look over any contract you sign so you are comfortable with all the terminology and there are no surprises.

Keep in mind there is a difference between lawyers and music lawyers. Music lawyers are typically much more familiar with the verbiage in music contracts because it's their specialty. If you need me to recommend one to you shoot me an email at coreybarker@hotmail.com.

# I am now signed up with a PRO. When and how do I get royalty checks?

*Royalty checks are only for those who are in line for the crown after the Queen of England passes. Sorry for the inconvenience and good luck choosing another dream.*

This seems to be everyone's favorite part. Tell me about the pay day.

Let's start with performance royalties. Performance royalties are a huge portion of a songwriter's income. They are generated by all broadcasts and public performances of your music and are paid quarterly to you and your publisher by your PRO.

1. Radio - each PRO has a slightly different way of figuring out which stations are playing which songs. Typically they will find out what a "Selected Few" stations are playing for a certain period of time and then estimate that as if "all" stations were doing the same. These stations are not normally given notice when this will be happening. They are only a small portion of the total stations out there but they usually have large markets.

It has been said that some record labels who practice the ancient art of "Payola" may find out which stations are on the list of "Selected Few" and accidentally send them a

Christmas card with a very large amount of Benjamin Franklins stuffed inside. Surely this doesn't really happen because that would not be fair to the smaller labels without bottomless pockets. That's probably just a silly rumor.

2. Television – Unlike radio "All" stations and Networks are required to keep logs of all of the music used during air time. This is a wonderfully clean way to keep track and make sure you are paid for your contributions without fail.

3. Movies – I hope you are sitting down for this. Let's say you have a song in the number one movie of the year shown on every screen in America. To figure out your performance royalty check simply calculate the number of screens by the number of tickets sold, add one million and them multiply all of that by a big fat goose egg.

Yep. You get not one penny in performance royalties for songs in movies. This makes about as much sense as making a sequel to Titanic but for some reason movie companies are able to get away with it. There can, however, be significant money involved in the sync license (see next section) so make sure your publisher fights for the fairest amount possible without losing the deal. Why did I end that sentence with "without losing the deal?" Here's another heart crusher for you.

Several years back I had a song that they wanted in a huge Christmas movie sequel. The movie company offered a wonderful amount of money (more than I make in a year at a good full time job). The person representing me asked them to increase the amount by $7,000 because there were two publishers and two writers involved that needed to be paid. They replaced our song the next day.

If I were negotiating I would have said, "How about you give us $3,000 less than you've offered and just remember us next time you're scoring a movie." My guess is they would have been impressed and we would have gotten that placement and many more. All I can say is poop.

4. Sync Fee - A sync fee refers to the compensation you will receive for the use of your song (audio component) synchronized with a visual component. They vary drastically per situation. Some publishers will grant a temporary sync license for no money at all simply for exposure though this is not recommended. In extreme cases such as a national commercial the song could annually generate well into the six figures if not seven. In both of these cases a specific time period may be set in the contract for your protection.

5. Mechanical Royalties – Mechanical Royalties are the royalties paid to you for the sale of records. The

statutory rate at the moment is 9.1 cents for your song per CD sold. This means if Garth Brooks sold 1 million copies of a song you wrote by yourself and you owned the publishing you would get a check for $91,000.

Your PRO is not responsible for this collection. The Harry Fox Agency is the most popular company in America for collecting royalties, paying publishers, auditing, etc. There are other smaller companies and some publishers even choose to collect themselves and save the 4.5 to 10% depending on what the outsourced collectors charge. I usually send my own mechanicals for indie artists but defer for the larger ones.

6. MUZAK is the music that you hear in elevators, grocery stores, etc. Song royalties for MUZAK are monitored by the PROS and you will get paid accordingly for that as well.

7. Internet Royalties – the internet may be the worst thing to ever happen to the music business in terms of song theft, but the PROS are starting to negotiate licenses for many internet music users. I do notice tiny additions to my BMI check from Press Play and similar organizations that are internet driven. Also iTunes and CDBaby are very legitimate ways of making money from your songs and getting proper payment.

8. Printed Music – Last but maybe least is sheet music. You also get paid for your music being placed in songbooks for choir, marching band, guitar lessons, etc.

# When do I need to copyright my song?

*Always copyright your song 12 years after it's a hit so you can't prove you wrote it. It brings great joy to most people as they argue it out in court while saying, "I promise I wrote it. You can ask my grandma but she died."*

It is usually a good idea to copyright your song before you start pitching it if you can afford to. You can download a form from the library of Congress. It can be expensive to pay $40 per song so many people fill up a CD and register the whole batch of songs together (i.e. Johnny's future hits volume 1, 2, etc). I recommend you do it this way so you don't have to take out a second mortgage on the home if you write frequently. The myth of "Poor Man's Copyright" (mailing a copy of your song and lyrics to yourself and never opening it) is a cute idea but there is no guarantee that will hold up in court. I have a shoe box full of those from the early 90's. Luckily all of those songs suck and I'm not too worried about it.

# Do I need to register my work before or after it's a hit?

*Six months after so you can keep everyone in suspense.*

It is EXTREMELY important that you register your work. Contrary to what you may believe your PRO does not magically know that you've created a song and that John Doe released it as a single. Make sure you go to the website for BMI, ASCAP or SESAC, whichever you belong to, and register the title, writers, publishers, percentages, and recording artist so you can enjoy the experience of going to the mailbox and collecting that big fat check that allows you to supersize your fries one day.

# When do I stop getting paid on my hit song?

September 32nd 2024.

After a certain point your song becomes public domain which means anyone can record it for free. So when is that point?

If it's a song you write today the answer is 70 years after you die. No, that does not mean they wire money to your casket, but your family can enjoy the fruits of your labor 70 years after you cross over. That's a sweet deal if you ask me. It's a sweet deal even if you don't ask me.

# How much can I make by writing a parody of a famous song?

*Enough to purchase 17 tacos, one rocking chair, 3 burping cloths and one camel who is addicted to nachos.*

Unfortunately the answer to that is usually jack squat unless you wrote the real song too.

In 2004 Lee Gibson and I wrote a parody of *Paint Me a Birmingham* called *Bake Me a Country Ham*. Country Comedian Cledus T Judd cut it less than two weeks later and it ended up being a hit single for him. We had to sign over our rights to the original publishers and never got a penny. It did however open a few doors for me that weren't open before and made the resume look better.

# How do I figure out what percentage of the song is mine if I wrote most of it and someone else helped out slightly?

*Divide the number of lines in the $2^{nd}$ verse by the height of your next door neighbor. Multiply that by how many times your grandpa goes to the bathroom during the middle of the night and then add that answer to the square root of 7.6. Finally, invert those numbers, count to four, and then sue the co-writers for $18.44 plus gas money for Twinkies.*

In almost all cases songs are simply split equally and not much math is needed. This is the way I always handle my co-writes. The idea is that you may write the majority today but the co-writer may write the majority of the next song and it all comes out in the wash.

There are instances where the old cliché is put into place. "Write a word – get a third." Many people use this in an instance where a song was basically finished but an outside writer came up with one tweak that made it better. If there is going to be a percentage split outside of the equal norm make sure all writers agree before the song is registered so there is no room for argument down the line.

# Does it make sense to search for an investor?

*Investors make no sense whatsoever. Studio time, instruments, gas for touring, merchandise, and advertising are all free.*

Every once in a blue moon the stars may align and a writer may find someone who believes in them enough to fund their publishing company for a percentage of the profits. There are many costs involved that your average person may not be able to afford that an investor could take care of:

1. DEMOS - A competitive demo can usually run from $500-$1000 per song.

2. DRAW/SALARY – If you are going to be writing full time you will need an income.

3. OFFICE – this is not 100 percent necessary but it looks more professional and allows you a place away from the distractions of home.

4. PLUGGER – assuming you don't have the cell numbers of all the major producers and labels you'll need to hire someone with a track record of getting songs placed on albums, TV shows, movies, etc.

5. INTERNET/ PHONE SERVICE.

6. COMPUTER (with printer for lyrics).

If you are going to quit your "real job" to chase this dream make sure that there is a guaranteed time limit in the contract. That way two months into the venture the investor can't say, "I changed my mind," and you are now unemployed and in need of a sandwich.

I have personally met with several investors over the years and most have been very flakey. Many seem to enjoy talking a big game but when it comes down to signing the checks to make it all happen they disappear faster than a joint at a Willie Nelson concert. I had one instance in 2005 where I had an investor lined up to put a quarter million behind an artist. On the day of signing he called twice saying he was stuck in traffic and running late but he'd be there shortly. He not only didn't show up but he never called again. That's good stuff.

# PART FIVE

## Do I Have What It Takes?

# What if I want to be a writer but I don't play an instrument or I'm great at music but I'm not naturally a lyricist?

*Then you might as well be a lion tamer who is afraid of whips. Sucks to be you.*

No problem. I know plenty of hit writers who don't even own a guitar or a piano and can't sing worth a lick. My dear late friend Alfons Kettner was one of the best melody guys on the planet but rarely wrote a word. He had one of the biggest R&B songs of all time *What You Won't Do For Love* recorded by Bobby Caldwell, Michael Bolton, Boys to Men, Aretha Franklin, sampled by Tupoc, etc. I used to love pushing record and turning him loose to see how many amazing licks or melodies he could come up with and then write the stories later down the line when time permitted.

That's the beauty of co-writing. Team up with someone who is strong in your weak areas and watch the magic happen. I have many musician friends that send me music. I often burn a CD, crank up the engine, and let the words pour out as I drive to work or wherever my destination may be. This is a great time management skill if you're short on time.

# What are the odds that I can make a living writing songs?

*93.7% so what are you waiting for, moron?*

If you want me to be brutally honest, the odds of you becoming rich from songwriting are equal to the odds of Chewbacca showing up to your next birthday party in a thong and break dancing with Barney the purple dinosaur while juggling six grenades, changing a baby's diaper, and singing I'm a Little Teapot with perfect annunciation.

However, the odds of us landing on the moon were astronomical (no pun intended). The odds of the Buffalo Bills losing four super bowls in a row were not any higher but it happened just the same.

My suggestion is to do the following:

1. Write the odds down on a sheet of paper.

2. Crumble said sheet of paper up.

3. Light that piece of paper on fire.

4. Find a new sheet of paper.

5. Write 100% down.

6. Stare at those odds until you believe it.

7. Continue writing and enjoy your journey.

# I haven't had any success and I've been at it for a while. When should I give up?

*Tomorrow at 2:00 after your lunch has settled.*

The answer is NEVER. If you truly love something you are disrespecting your heart by quitting, unless of course it's crack.

There is no guarantee that success, however you define it, will come quickly or ever but a wise man once said you never fail until you stop trying. Insert any similar clichés you would like to after that and it doesn't make them any less true. If you write every day and incorporate the art of re-writing/tweaking, you can't help but become better. It's impossible not to.

If everyone you know says you're terrible then perhaps you shouldn't spend a zillion dollars demoing up everything you've ever written, but that doesn't mean you need to stop trying to get better if you love to write. One day you could make them eat their words and politely offer them a beer to wash it down.

# PART SIX

# What Technical Terms Do I Need To Know?

# What does it mean if I get a song "on hold"?

*The artist enjoys the texture of the CD cover so they want to hold it in their hand and perhaps snuggle with it for a while.*

In the old days if you had a song on hold it meant the artist who chose it is planning on cutting it on their next album and requesting that you not pitch it to anyone else until that happens. These days it can mean a few things:

1. Exactly what it used to mean.

2. It has peaked the artist's or producer's interest and they'd like to keep it for further consideration (but no guarantees).

3. It is very similar to one they already want to release and they'd like to pretend like they like yours so you will stop pitching it until their song is already out. This is quite dirty, but it does happen and there's not much you can do about it.

I suggest you celebrate all your holds "cautioumistically", meaning optimistically but with caution, like I do.

# What is a single song contract?

*When your writing is so atrocious that it makes people want to jump off a cliff and end the pain as quickly as possible, so the citizens of your home town may pool all their money together and offer you a single song contract. This is a payoff contract that says you will never again write a single song as long as you live.*

A single song contract is offered when a publisher believes in a particular song you wrote and wants to pitch it. It does not include any future or past song you have nor is it a promise of a staff deal hence the term "single song." You will probably be offered a few of these before a staff deal ever presents itself. As long as the publisher is reputable and there is a reversion clause, this contract is usually a good thing.

"Reversion clause" means that after a specified amount of time of no action the song reverts back to you. Two or three year reversion clauses are quite common. This protects the writer from signing over their song and the publisher simply sitting on it.

# What are Sharks?

*Duh....did you not see Jaws?*

Unfortunately there are many people in the business who make their living conning aspiring writers and singers. These precious music business bottom feeders are called sharks. In many cases they will overcharge you to do demos with them, charge you an overly large "consulting" fee, or tell you they can make you famous for (insert ridiculous dollar amount here). Most will lead you to believe that you are the greatest thing since sliced bread even if you suck harder than a two year old with a supersized slurpy.

Sharks can come in the form of producers, publishers, advisors, indie labels, networks, managers, pluggers and more. There are more honest people than crooks in my experience but it pays to be aware that they are out there. When in doubt always research the person or group.

# What is a work tape and how is it different form a demo?

*Work tape is any roll of duct or scotch tape that you did not have to pay for because you stole it from the place you work at. This differs from a demo because a demo is more about music and tape is used for holding things together.*

When you're writing session is over, whether the song is finished or not, you will want to make a recording of the song for reference. This is called a "work tape." Work tapes are simply a quick recording of your song so you will not forget the melody or phrasing. After you have worked out all the kinks and your song is ready to demo you will want to make a final work tape with all the revisions. This is what will be sent to the producer as reference for the demo. Make sure the guitar or piano is easy to hear so they don't have to guess at your chords. I made that mistake last night as a matter of fact.

# I heard a writer talking about writing up. What does that mean?

*"Writing up" is when a few co-writers book a flight and write a song as the plane is lifting off. When the plane stops climbing and levels off you have to stop because the lane is no longer going up. If you have not finished at that point you have to book another flight and try again.*

Writing Up is the term given when you book a co-write with someone who is more experienced than yourself. It is basically writing with a mentor. This is highly recommended if you get the chance as you can't help but learn when you hang out with people who are masters of the craft. Keep in mind they may not gain much out of helping you, so always be grateful for their time when they choose to give you a chance.

I also recommend marrying up if you ever get the chance. Not sure what my wife got out of it, but she sure makes me look good.

# PART SEVEN

## How Can I Hold On To My Dream?

# Should I set goals or just write and see what happens?

*I would suggest that you fly by the seat of your pants. However, I fear that I may be sued by someone who lives in a nudist colony and doesn't own any pants. I simply don't have time to go to court nor the money to buy anyone pants so I'll advise you to set goals instead.*

Name any business where the company does not set goals annually, monthly, or even weekly. Assuming you'd like to be a successful money making songwriter you shouldn't treat your business any differently. For years I set monthly goals and calculated the percentages that I actually achieved. It helped me keep my focus and I was better able to reach my annual goals.  Here are some examples of some simple annual goals you could set that could help you:

1. Get a song cut.

2. Pitch at least one song every week.

3. Join a songwriter's organization.

4. Write 100 songs.

5. Write with 10 people I've never worked with before.

6. Get my catalog in order (burn a CD and print a lyric sheet of every song I've written thus far).

7. Demo x amount of songs this year.

8. Pitch a song for someone else that I didn't write. (this is a good karma builder).

9. Subscribe to rowfax.com or another pitch sheet so I know who's cutting and when.

10. Contact up-and-coming artists about co-writing or at least submitting some of your songs for their future projects.

I normally set at least 20 annual goals but I may have a monthly goal/to-do list in addition to that.

# What is a Retreat?

*A songwriters' retreat is when you realize the writer next to you is much more talented so you run as fast as you can in the opposite direction and bury your head in a hole.*

Songwriters' retreats are getaways where you can focus on nothing but writing. A change of scenery can be very helpful sometimes. Grab a few of your songwriter buddies and head to a cabin, a lake, a beach, a shack, or find a place inside one of Shaquille O'Neal's shoes and spend a few days participating in a song-athon. There are several ways you can make this interesting:

1. Challenge yourselves to reach a goal (e.g. number of songs written).

2. Focus on a certain project (e.g. Christmas songs, kids' songs, up-tempo female, etc.)

3. Take turns coming up with titles.

4. Take each song in a different direction than you had planned without changing the title.

5. Insist that no two tempos can be the same.

6. Write for as many different genres as possible (pop, reggae, country, Christian, polka, etc.)

7. Every time you suggest a line that everyone rejects you have to take a shot of...apple juice or whatever your beverage may be.

You can even take a retreat by yourself for some peace of mind and see how you can get your creative juices flowing.

I spend all my free time trying to make it happen and often get frustrated as success seems so improbable. What do I do?

*Open up the nearest window and shout out, "I am a loser." Then immediately take up a new hobby such as underwater basket weaving or perhaps open a ballet dance club for left handed hairy men over the age of 80.*

One thing that has worked to keep me motivated as I'm reaching for the major prize has been rewarding myself for little accomplishments along the way. Here are a few examples:

1. I used to frame every cut I got and hang it on the wall (no matter how small). This was my way of thanking the artist who thought enough of my song to include it on their album, but it also helped remind me that somebody cares and *I am* making progress. Eventually I ran out of room on both my walls in the living room. The funny thing was that the plaques for the CD's often cost more than the royalty checks from the cuts.

2. Treat yourself to your favorite dinner as a reward for each cut.

3. The cheapest reward may be to simply take a picture of yourself holding the CD and make a scrap book.

A small victory is still a victory. Use that accomplishment for motivation as you climb the next rung up the ladder of success.

# I have writer's block. Any suggestions?

*No. That just means you are creatively challenged. Good luck chilling in Averageville for the rest of your life and may the Good Lord have mercy on your soul.*

Writer's block is going to happen from time to time. Don't worry. Here are a few tips when it sneaks up on you:

1. Get some rest and try again later. Sometimes we are just simply too exhausted for our brains to be creative.

2. Watch one of your favorite sitcoms or dramas and challenge yourself to pick out a title from something they say in that episode.

3. Exercise! Getting the blood pumping is a good way to energize your mind.

4. Take the track from a song you have already written and write a completely different melody and lyric to it. That way you get double the chance of having a hit without having to pay for a new track. If you do this make sure the co-writer from the original gives you permission and still gets credit if there was one.

5. Call a co-writer and ask if they have any ideas they'd like to work on with you

6. Pick up a guitar and start strumming until a melody kicks in.

7. Choose a significant event in your life and then write about it but with the opposite outcome.

8. Make up a word or character that doesn't exist and write a song about it or him.

The most important thing when you get stuck is to remember not to force it. Don't try to finish it just to be done and settle with an average or overused line. It's better to have one terrific song than ten acceptable songs.

# When can I tell everyone about my cut?

Just got the news Snoop Dog and George Strait are Recording my song. When can I post it on Facebook and scream it from the roof tops?

*Right away. Go ahead and buy a Porsche and a house boat as quick as you can too.*

Please, for the love of God, don't announce anything until you can go buy it at Wal-Mart or online. I can't tell you how many times I had a song "on hold" that either didn't get cut or got cut and left off the album. In some cases they were artists that would have contributed to an early retirement for me. In other instances an artist may switch producers and go a different direction with their music, or they could lose funding all together and the album never happens.

I remember how excited I was when I got an email from a major artist's wife saying that my song was going to be the title song for their retirement album. This particular legend passed away before the recording date, and I had already told my family the great news at Thanksgiving.

In another instance I had a huge country artist personally text my plugger "the day of" the recording session to remind him to email the lyrics for my two songs that were going on his Christian CD. We were doing back flips until the CD came out and my songs were not on it.

# My song is ready to come to life. Who should I choose to demo it?

*It doesn't matter who you choose. Your incomparable musical brilliance will be able to shine through the worst engineer's boo boo's, so just pick the cheapest one and wait for Garth Brooks to call.*

That is a difficult question to answer if I don't know where you live. Let's start by saying there are very few places outside of Nashville that I would personally trust (although there are exceptions of course). The good thing is you don't have to live in Nashville to get a Nashville Demo. Most studios will let you mail them the work tape, and they can mail you the finished product shortly after.

Make sure your phrasing is exactly like you want it on the work tape before you send it in! Odds are the demo singer will mimic you and copy any mistakes you may have accidentally made. I've had this happen a few times and it makes me want to pull my hair out. Both of them!

I prefer to use Ohana Music Group whenever I can. I discovered them in 2000 and have rarely spent a dollar elsewhere. As a matter of fact I took a second job for a few years and signed over every penny to the CEO Kimo Forrest so I could build my catalog of demos up. As luck would have it Ohana Music Group eventually became an indie label as well, and I continue to get several cuts each year through them. Feel free to check them out at:

Ohanamusicgroup.com

Email : (ohanamusicgroup@yahoo.com)

Other producers/companies I could recommend for your demos: Kent Wells, Kenny Royster, Century Music Group, Skidd Mills, Jim Cartwright, Aerugo Productions, and a few more I could mention, but I need to go to the bathroom right now so I have to stop typing.

Don't forget no matter who you use to produce...hiring that top notch vocalist to put the icing on the cake is a must!

# Should I play my songs at writer's nights?

*Yes, but play them in Spanish while wearing a sombrero and eating a burrito so you will stand out from the other writers.*

Songwriter's nights are a good way to showcase your talents and meet new people who share the same goals. In many cases they have led to staff deals as a publisher happened to be there scouting that night.

On the flip side you have to be very careful which songs you play. Often there are other writers searching for good hooks and they may steal yours, re-write them, and get them cut before you have a chance to demo or pitch yours.

Remember you can't copyright a title. That's why I usually don't play my most creative titles out until they are cut. I normally go with something funny to give something different to the crowd.

# Would it be helpful for me to join a writer's organization?

*No. You already know everything so it's more beneficial to join a weight loss club. They may need a catchy theme song called* Put Down That Donut *and who better qualified to write it than a six time BMI songwriter of the year like yourself.*

There are many writers' organizations that exist to serve you such as Tennessee Songwriter's Association International (TSAI), Nashville Songwriters Association, etc.

I would recommend you join one or all if you're schedule will allow it. I have been a part of most of them and I currently serve on the Board of Directors at TSAI. These organizations offer critique nights, networking opportunities, workshops, as well as chances to pitch your songs to artists and labels while you witness their reactions. The later of those reasons seems to be the biggest draw for most writers aspiring to get that elusive cut they've been dreaming of.

Most of these organizations also have an end of the year awards banquet where you could have an opportunity to win awards and get recognition for your hard work and dedication. This may not be equivalent to a Grammy but it can do wonders for your confidence. "Award Winning Songwriter" before your name doesn't look too shabby on a pitch either.

# I need to concentrate on my music. It's not possible to work a real job and still write songs is it?

*No it's not possible. On average it can take 5-10 years to get your first cut. Before you move to Nashville eat 7 buffets and this should last you for all the years you are not employed and unable to buy food. No problem.*

It's not only possible but it is mandatory for over 99% of writers today unfortunately. I'm aware of several writers with big hits in the past who have had to start waiting tables to make up the difference in their pay cuts from the publishing deals they had. Due to internet piracy the revenues are not coming in like they used to for album cuts thus publishing companies can't pay out what they want to as draws. In many cases the draw has dwindled down to a 3$^{rd}$ of what the writers used to make.

Last year I worked a full time job for US Community Credit Union and still wrote 150 songs. Sometimes it's wise to lean on the strength and/or free time of your co-writers. For instance I may write a lyric before work or at night before I go to bed and email it to a melody co-writer of mine. Often by the time I get home from work they have written the melody, sang it on a work tape, and the mp3 is waiting for me in my inbox. I love it when that happens.

On the flip side a music writer could send me some music, and I put a lyric to it when the kids go to sleep and send it back to them. The key in either one of those cases is a mixture of concentration, time management, and ability to not ignore your family in the process. Not easily done but an understanding wife/husband can make a huge difference and I am truly blessed in that regard. (I love Kristina Barker!!!)

You could also work a breakfast shift as a waiter or night shift as a bartender. This would free up your days for writing appointments and I see this happen with a huge percentage of writers.

The point is writers find a way to write. Not just because we want to but because we have to. It's in our blood. I've heard people say "you're a sellout" if you get a real job and don't blindly chase the dream. I call horse poop on that. What you are is responsible, rational and logical and in no way does it make you less of a dreamer.

Speaking of which…..I would like to thank the Marriott and the US Community Credit Union for the collective 21 years they have supported my dream and let me off work when opportunities arrived. I would highly recommend working for either of these companies while chasing your goals down.

PART EIGHT

What About TV Shows, Movies and

Youtube?

# What is a TV track?

*It's a railroad track where everyone tosses their old television sets because they are not compatible with Comcast high definition.*

A "TV track" is simply the music to your song with the background vocals included but not the lead vocals. If you are a lyricist and a singer but don't play an instrument these could come in handy for you in many live performance venues. Most people can't afford to hire a band and background singers for television performances so keeping TV tracks from your demo sessions is a great idea as well.

# How do I get my song in a TV show or movie?

*Give it to Betty White because she knows everybody!*

When it comes to television and movies music supervisors are the gatekeepers. The music supervisor is in charge of scoring the music for the footage. There are opportunities for full songs, snippets of songs, instrumentals, ambiance music etc.

If you do not personally know a music supervisor, or a plugger who can get to one, then Google can be your best friend. In many cases a music supervisor is scoring for several TV shows at a time. If you are lucky enough to befriend one then it's backflip time.

When it comes to movies often times the studio has an in-house production team that creates all their music, but there are exceptions to the rule. Movie trailers or special scenes have been known to use a popular pop/rock song to draw people in.

When I did the sound track for *Birth of a Legend,* I sat down with the Music Supervisor in Alabama and he played scene by scene for me. I went through my catalog and played a few things for each scene, and he ultimately chose what he wanted. Normally they will just describe a scene or tell you the style they are looking for in an email and you take your best guess as you mp3 it. I was spoiled in my scenario.

If you are blessed with a publishing deal then your publisher likely has a working relationship with at least one and will take that burden of tracking down a Music Supervisor off your hands. The PRO will also negotiate the licensing fee for you. "Simply Grand Music" out of Memphis and "Laura Lynn Entertainment" in Nashville have been very instrumental in my TV success as a writer. I would definitely recommend reaching out to them if you don't already know someone.

# Can I make money off of my YouTube videos?

*No, unless you don't mind riding a Harley naked off a ramp with a chicken on your head through a ring of fire to the tune of "Another one bites the dust" in front of a screaming crowd of elderly blind Eskimos.*

Yes, it is possible to make money on Youtube if you click the monetize button before you post. However four things could get you in trouble and negate your payment:

1. You don't own the rights to the song you posted.

2. You don't own the pictures you posted to the slide show video.

3. You don't own the video footage.

4. Your name is Bob and your mother hates cheese.

*Ok maybe only the first three things are true.

I would not look to get rich from any videos you post, but the exposure can potentially be amazing.

Anything like this or any other social media outlet that you can use which gives you free publicity is definitely worth trying. A few singers have been discovered that way and it cost them nothing.

# 10 WAYS TO MAKE MONEY OFF YOUTUBE

1 - Capitalize off meta data. Meta data refers to the title, tags, and description of your video. You want to make it as easy as possible for someone to find you when they are looking for you. Better yet…you want to make it where people accidentally stumble upon you as they are looking for similar videos. For instance, if you have a funny song about eating yogurt you don't just want to tag it with "yogurt."

You may try tagging yogurt song, funny fruit song, best song ever, funniest song ever, you have to hear this, lol song, weird al should have recorded this song, I'm dying laughing, epic yogurt song, etc. (Not that I can imagine a yogurt song being very funny.)


2 – Use it to send traffic to your website for purchase of your product (cd/book,etc.). Do live videos of you playing a song that can be found on your cd. Include the link to purchase in the description your videos.


2 - Make a video promoting your product. Talk about some of the highlights and industry praise and, again, include the link to purchase.

3 – Create a web TV series. Start your own reality show, so to speak, that creates interest in you and provides updates. Maybe include live video updates before or after a gig. Possibly post hype after you have just written the best song ever with Elton John. Cash Creek TV is a good example of webisodes from bands. Songwriters can do the same.

4 - Become a youtube star. The rumors say pay is between $2.50 and $7.00 per thousand views for youtube stars, so entertain!

5 - The youtube partner program has a monetize button. You definitely want to click on that. Once again make sure you own all the pics, footage, and music in the video so there are no issues with infringement.

6 – Use a cute kid, animal, puppet, etc. to market your product in the video. The world loves cuteness, and cuteness leads to more views. More views leads to more money. More money leads to happy you!

7- Test market your product. Ask your audience about suggestions on how to make it better, which parts you should leave out or change.

Which songs should be the single? What questions the book should answer that it hasn't already? Which video is the fan favorite? etc.

Free advice never hurts!

8 – Make a Tutorial. Show people how you wrote the song, how you researched your info for the book, how you came up with the script for the video, mistakes that you learned from, etc. People like to be informed and educated.

9 – Be funny!!!!!  I never met anyone that didn't like to laugh. When you find something that tickles your funny bone you are inclined to share. When you share, a bigger audience will see the video which will have your link to purchase in it. You can guess what happens after that.

10 – Cross promote your youtube page using your Facebook, email, and every other social media that allows. This is all free advertising that didn't exist a few short years ago, so take advantage of every way you can think of to drive traffic to your youtube channel.

# IN CLOSING

Remember this is not a race. Nothing big happens overnight that I've ever been able to witness. If you get discouraged easily this may not be the business for you. When I moved to town in 1998 I was told that the average writer or artist stayed in town for eight months and then moved back home after they saw how hard it was. At that time there were an estimated 100,000 songwriters in this city alone. I wouldn't be surprised if that number has doubled or tripled today. On this particular roller coaster you will have many "DOWNS" before you get to the "UPs" but you can't let that stop you. The longer you are kept out of the winners' circle the more time you will have to build up your catalog and have an arsenal of hit songs in the waiting when your number is called. Patience is not just a virtue, it's a must.

When the frustration kicks in ask yourself this question: Who appreciates a hit song more...Guy Number 1 who has lived in Nashville only two months before Rascal Flats cuts his song...or Guy Number 2 who was here trying and trying for a decade or two before the skies finally parted and his bread winning song was born? This book is most certainly written from the standpoint of Guy Number 2.

Believe in yourself, believe in your dream, and NEVER GIVE UP!

Best of luck in your career,

Corey Lee Barker

# ABOUT THE AUTHOR

Corey Lee Barker was born in Grandview, Texas and grew up in Memphis, Tennessee. He was writing stories, joke books, and poems as soon as he could hold a pencil and eventually wrote his first serious song at the age of 13. By the mid 90's he was getting frequent radio play on Froggy '94 and Kix 106 radio stations with his comedy songs and ended up having several of his songs published by Simply Grand Music. He moved to Nashville in 1998 to pursue his dream. He's been a staff writer for SGM, Nashville Records, Artist Development Network, Stockbridge Records, and March Music.

To this date he has racked up over 400 cuts on artist albums including Daryle Singletary, Cledus T Judd, Rebecca Lynn Howard, T.G. Shephard, Johnny Lee, Jason Jones, and Bill Anderson. He has co-written music for the hit TV shows *Smallville* and *The Messengers*, the theme songs for *Last Chance Highway* on Animal Planet, *Tom's Wild Life* on GAC, scored the entire sound track for the independent comedy movie *Birth of a Legend*, and landed a song on the Grammy winning album *Come Share The Wine* in 2007.

*Medal of Honor* co-written with Lucas Hoge, is also the theme song for Wrangler National Patriot.

Corey currently has a working relationship with several of Nashville's publishing companies, record labels, production companies, hit writers, pluggers, and recording artists.

In the past two years he has been nominated for Songwriter of the Year by the Tennessee Songwriters Association, Inspirational Country Music Association, and North American Country Music Association.

In 2012 he took his first venture as producer and created a children's' inspirational album entitled *United We Sing* which can be purchased on Itunes and cdbaby as well as selected churches in the Nashville area. Each song is co-written by Corey and sung by some of Nashville's finest child voices. Check it out if you get a chance.

Facebook.com/unitedwesingalbum

# Other Frequently Asked Questions

**What was your funniest songwriting moment?**

I was making a work tape for Dolly Parton's producer Kent Wells years ago. The song was going to be recorded the next day so I had to finish quickly. I was 20 seconds away from finishing the recording when my roommate walked into the room and farted. It sounded like King Kong stepped on a duck. I somehow made it through the rest of the song without busting out laughing until I hit the stop button. I couldn't find it in my heart to redo the work tape because it was too funny and I sent it just as it was. I would have given anything to see Kent's face when he heard it. Out of respect for my former roommate's privacy I won't tell you his name was Keith Burgess.

**How many writers have you written with over the years?**

It's never taken me over a year to write with any writer. Usually we are done in two hours or less.

**If you could write with any writer, dead or alive...who would it be?**

I'm not very stoked about writing with dead writers. They never contribute anything and it's difficult to get them to sign the publishing contracts if something big happens with the song.

### What was the worst moment in your career?

There was a girl in college that I thought was beautiful and I wanted to get her attention. I wrote her a song called *I've Got an Angel*. The following Saturday I was playing an acoustic show at "Crazy Larry's" in Memphis. I couldn't wait to debut the song as I saw her in the crowd. I closed my eyes and let it rip (the song....not a fart). As I finished the first chorus I opened my eyes to see if she was staring at me, and I saw her making out with another guy on the dance floor. What a wonderful moment for my ego!

Coming in second place would be the time I got fired from a place that I was playing for free.

### You've had a great deal of TV success writing with country star Lucas Hoge including music on the hit show *Smallville*, the theme song for *Tom's Wild Life* on GAC, and the theme song for *Last Chance Highway* on Animal Planet. How did you guys meet?

A mutual friend of ours was having a small get together at her house in 2004 and invited us both. As the evening progressed we ended up out on the back deck passing the guitar around and swapping stories. When it came Lucas's turn he said, "You guys have to hear this song. It's going be my single one day."

When he said it's called *Day Over Beautiful* my heart just sunk and I was almost angry at him, myself, and the world. I had just written a song by that title and I thought it was completely original, and I would make a million one day when it was recorded by the right artist. I told him that and he said, "It's not going to be better than this one" and I could see his future wife agreeing as he picked up the guitar. He was right. It wasn't better. It was the exact same song.

Apparently my co-writer Jody Harris had given it to him. Lucas and I have been good buddies ever since. He was even one of the four best men in my wedding.

**Who was the nicest star you've ever worked with?**

I'd have to say it's a tie between T.G. Shephard and John Michael Montgomery. I actually met Elvis when I was two years old but I can't remember it very well. My dad said he was very kind though.

**What is your proudest moment as a writer so far?**

After a heartwarming call from the Sangre de Cristo Hospice in Colorado, Lucas Hoge and I had the privilege of writing a song with Natalie Fognani. She passed away from Lou Gehrig's disease less than a year later. The fact that we got to fulfill Natalie's dying wish or that the song went to #2 on power source charts for inspirational country was only part of the blessing.

Lucas had someone tell him that they were on their way home to commit suicide when they heard our song on the radio and changed their mind. There is no award or financial blessing that could ever compare with the amazing feeling of knowing something you took part in actually saved someone's life.

Having a song on my favorite TV show, *Smallville*, did not hurt my feelings either.

**If you could get one of your songs recorded by any artist/s who would it be?**

Weird Al Yankovic, Randy Travis, Garth Brooks, George Strait, Blake Shelton, and Alabama (not necessarily in that order).

**What's the biggest money maker you've written thus far?**

Stockbridge Records recording artist Barry Michael and I wrote a song called *Heroes And Angels* in 2009. After making its debut as the theme song for the World War II Veterans conference at Caesar's Palace it got picked up by a national sponsor of the military. They leased the song for a year and sent us a fat check every month. I was able to make many long overdue house improvements, book a few vacations, and put a nice diamond ring on my wife's finger.

**What was the first song of yours anyone put out as a single on radio?**

*Hello Beer* by Lloyd Knight was a single in 2003. I was lucky enough to get to go on the radio tour with him, and we had a blast. It charted on the music row charts but not Billboard. I'm hoping the song gets another shot one day.

**If it was your turn to have the next big hit and you were allowed to let another overdue writer take your place who would it be?**

Either Jody Harris or Rick Tiger. They've been in town longer than I have and can write with the best of them. Not to mention they are fantastic guys to boot.

**Which writer have you co-written the most songs with?**

Anita Cox. I believe we've written over 150 songs together. I nicknamed her "Mrs. Melody" years ago because her musical ideas never stop.

**You've written with multiple recording artists. If you owned a record label and had limitless money which acts that you've worked with would you sign?**

Cash Creek, Lucas Hoge, Due West, Kree Harrison, and Joey Hyde.

**Best surprise moment of your career?**

Lance Wing and I were invited to the recording session for Jimmy Sturr's album a few years back. Jimmy won the Grammy for polka about 14 times in a row. He said he had a guest vocalist cutting our song on the record. That vocalist turned out to be Bill Anderson backed by the Jordanaires (Elvis's background singers). We were very blessed to watch them work together that day.

**Current show you wish you could write a song for?**

*The Walking Dead.* My wife and I watch every episode at least three times.

**When you first moved to town, how long did you expect to have to wait for your first number one hit?**

No more than two years. I was a moron.

**First number one writer you ever wrote with?**

Troy Martin. I actually worked with him at the Courtyard by Marriott for a while.

**Favorite era of country singers you wish you could write for?**

The 90's without a doubt: Garth Brooks, George Strait, Alan Jackson, Clay Walker, Clint Black, Mark Chestnut, Tracy Lawrence, Joe Diffie, John Michael Montgomery...need I say more? I miss the hat act era.

**If you could freeze frame a moment in your career and put it in a picture...which moment would you choose?**

I actually have that picture. In 2012, I put together an inspirational kids' album called *United We Sing*. I had worked on the songs for several years prior and looked forward to the day I could see it come together. That moment when I had 20 kids in the studio singing the chorus of the theme song at the same time was priceless. I have pictures and memories from that day that I will cherish forever.

You are more than welcome to buy a copy on Itunes or cdbaby by the way. A portion of the proceeds go to parentingspecialneeds.org

**You went from dreaming that someone would cut one of your songs in college to having multiple cuts every year. To what or whom do you attribute that success to?**

God. Period. None of us have the ability to give birth to ourselves much less manifest a talent out of thin air. How much time we put into honing that skill, however, is up to us. Practice, patience, prayer and faith in yourself can serve as an unstoppable combination of weapons in the fight for recognition. I incorporate all four in everything I do.

# NOTES

# NOTES

# NOTES

Made in the USA
Lexington, KY
03 August 2015